CHAPTER 1

INTRODUCTION

In the spring of 1958, while assigned as an Associate Professor of Military Science and Tactics at the University of Florida, the writer studied international politics. The importance of the role of the armed forces in American diplomacy was apparent early in the program. The military was an instrument which could be used to impose the will of the United States upon another nation when other means had either failed or been discarded. The desire to determine the true role of the United States armed forces in foreign politics resulted in the selection of the subject for this thesis.

Karl von Clausewitz stated: "We see . . . that war is not merely a political act but a real political instrument, a continuation of political intercourse, a carrying out of the same by other means."[1] Is the role of the military in the foreign politics of the United States a continuation of diplomacy by another means, or is the military an integral part of the diplomatic team of the nation? Has the importance of the armed forces in foreign policy increased as the United States developed; and, if so, what were the causes? The purpose of this thesis is to study the use of the armed forces in selected periods of history and attempt to determine the answer to these questions.

---

[1]Karl von Clausewitz, On War, p. 16.

1

This thesis will discuss the War of 1812 and the involvement of the United States in the struggle between the power nations of Europe, Great Britain, and France. Next will be a study of the Spanish American war and the events leading to the war, to be followed by a discussion of World War I and World War II. A brief look at the post World War II period, including international organizations, international actions of the United States, and the Korean War, will complete the historical study.

Based upon the conclusions derived from the study of the historical periods listed, this thesis will attempt to evaluate the contribution made to the art of foreign diplomacy during each period. The evaluation will not encompass the normal use of the military to close with and destroy the enemy, but will concentrate on the employment of the power of the armed forces in peaceful negotiations short of war.

CHAPTER 2

WAR OF 1812

Captain Alfred T. Mahan, in his Sea Power in Its Relations to the War of 1812, stated:

> The two principal immediate causes of the War of 1812 were the impressment of seamen from American merchant ships, upon the high seas, to serve in the British Navy, and the interference with the carrying trade of the United States by the naval power of Great Britain.[1]

These have been accepted by historians as the primary causes of the War of 1812, but there were other causes which contributed to the outbreak of hostilities. The frontiersmen blamed the British for supplying the Northwest Indians with supplies, the "War Hawk" faction in Congress regarded Canada as a desirable possession of great value to the United States, and the Westerners blamed the British for the serious depression which existed because of the loss of overseas markets.[2]

The War of 1812 was the most unusual war in the history of the United States. The absence of a rapid means of communication between Great Britain and the United States contributed to the war. A few days before the United States declared war on Great Britain in June of 1812, the British government had stated that it would revoke the provisions of the Orders in Council which applied to the United

---

[1]Alfred T. Mahan, Sea Power in Its Relations to the War of 1812, Vol. 1, p. 2.
　　[2]Thomas A. Bailey, A Diplomatic History of the American People, pp. 136-139.

States.[3] These particular laws provided for the blockade of the European coast by the Royal Navy, and, from the standpoint of the United States, interrupted a very lucrative trade with the European nations.[4] If the information that the British government was repealing its despicable laws had been available in America, it is reasonable to assume that Congress would not have declared war on Great Britain, and the United States would not have become involved in the French and British confrontation.

Except for a period of approximately eighteen months between 1801 and 1803, Great Britain and France had been at war since 1793. Both nations needed supplies from their colonies, and the United States was in a good position to transport these supplies from the British and French West Indies to Europe. The value of trade carried by United States shipping increased fourfold from 1790 to 1806.[5] The United States was getting rich on the war in Europe, and the implementation of the Orders in Council by the British presented a formidable barrier to the continued development of the American foreign trade. Both France and Great Britain interfered with American shipping which attempted to supply both countries, and both nations reacted to the actions of the other nation.

---

[3]Mahan, op. cit., p. 276.
[4]Eli F. Heckscher, The Continental System, pp. 114-121.
[5]Ibid., pp. 101-104.

FRENCH INFLUENCE

Early in 1805, Napoleon I abandoned his plans to invade Great Britain, and decided to conquer the continent of Europe. This proved to be a good decision for the British Navy destroyed the French and Spanish fleets at the Battle of Trafalgar in October of the same year, and Napoleon had no invasion shipping available.[6] During the next two years, Great Britain and France both implemented a series of blockades and counterblockades which were designed to destroy the economy of the other.

The British blockade and Orders in Council of 1807 required neutral nations to clear all goods through Great Britain prior to delivery to the continent. The French Decree of Berlin (1806) and Decree of Milan (1807) blockaded British shipping from the continent, and provided for French seizure of neutral ships which traded with Great Britain, or permitted the British inspection rights.[7] This placed the United States, the leading power carrying colonial goods to Europe, directly between the two powers. When the United States shipping complied with the British regulations, France seized the ships as they reached port on the continent. Ships which complied with French decrees were seized by the British.

Both France and Great Britain inflicted severe losses on American shipping; however, France seized ships when they landed at European ports while the British boarded American shipping on

---

[6]Bradford Perkins, Prologue to War, p. 3.
[7]Heckscher, op. cit., pp. 81-105, 389-408.

5

the high seas. The United States objected to this violation of international waters, but the British maintained that they were searching for British citizens who had deserted their country. Many of the sailors on American ships were former British sailors; however, numerous American citizens were impressed into the British Navy as a result of the enforcement of the blockades.[8]

To perfect his continental system of keeping all British shipping blockaded from the continent of Europe, Napoleon I conquered Portugal in 1807. This nation, friendly with Great Britain for years, had not complied with Napoleon's decrees of no trade with the British. Naploeon followed this success with an attack on Spain. The Spanish requested assistance from Great Britain, and in the summer of 1808 Britain became involved in the Peninsular War which lasted for the next five years.[9] The majority of the British Army was occupied in the conduct of this war; however, a few veterans were available to participate in the small war in America. A considerable portion of the Royal Navy was employed against the United States.[10] Thus the lack of land forces to reinforce the British Army already operating in America contributed to the final victory for the United States.

[8]Alfred L. Burt, The United States, Great Britain and British North America, pp. 220-222.

[9]George Rude, Revolutionary Europe, 1783-1815, pp. 264-268.

[10]R. Ernest Dupuy and Trevor N. Dupuy, Military Heritage of America, p. 126.

THE BRITISH POSITION

Great Britain did not want war with the United States in 1812. This was evidenced by the revocation of the Orders in Council in 1812 when it became apparent that continued enforcement against the shipping of the United States would lead to war.[11]

To understand fully the reluctance of Great Britain to allow American shipping access to the European continent, one should view the situation through British eyes. Great Britain dominated the sea with her powerful navy; however, powerful as it was, the navy could not be used on the continent of Europe where Napoleon dominated all Europe with his powerful Army. British trade was seriously damaged by the continental system established by Napoleon. British shipping could not land on the continent, and the export of goods from England to the continent had virtually ceased. When the shipping of neutral nations supplied France with produce, Great Britain intervened and terminated the operation. Great Britain could not permit shipment of essential goods to an enemy from neutral nations. The British believed that nations carrying goods directly to France were allies of the enemy.[12]

Great Britain and France increased their attacks on American shipping, and the United States reacted by passing the Embargo Act of 1807. This act terminated all American commerce with foreign countries, and resulted in increased British animosity against the

---

[11]Henry Adams, History of the United States, Vol. VI, p. 286.
[12]Burt, op. cit., pp. 222-224, 254-255.

7

United States.[13] The Embargo Act was repealed by the Nonintercourse Act of 1809. This allowed commercial trade with all nations except France and Great Britain, and authorized the United States to resume trade with either France or Great Britain on an individual basis when they discontinued the violation of the rights of American neutral shipping.[14] In May, 1810, the United States passed the Macon Act. This provided for the resumption of trade with France and Great Britain upon the expiration of the Nonintercourse Act, but it contained provision for termination of trade with either country in event the other revoked its restrictive regulations against the United States.[15]

President Madison honored a French claim that their restriction had been lifted, and in November, 1810, notified the British that the United States intended to implement the nonintercourse law against Great Britain in February, 1811, unless the Orders in Council were revoked. The British, convinced that the French Decrees of Berlin and Milan had not been revoked by Napoleon, did not comply with the American demand. The British were correct in their suspicion of Napoleon, and the Americans had been deceived. The French continued to detain and capture American shipping in the ports of continental Europe.[16]

---

[13]Adams, op. cit., Vol. IV, p. 175.
[14]Ibid., pp. 432-453.
[15]Mahan, op. cit., p. 234.
[16]Adams, op. cit., Vol. V, pp. 338-344.

In view of the foregoing, the British refusal to discontinue the Orders in Council was justified. The United States was aiding the French by transporting supplies to continental ports and terminating all commercial trade with Great Britain.

MILITARY OPERATIONS

Anti-British sentiment grew as Great Britain continued to seize American shipping and impress American citizens into the Royal Navy. Difficulty with the Indians in the Northwest was also blamed on the British in Canada, and the United States declared war on Great Britain on 18 June, 1812.[17] There had been a continuous threat of war with either France or Great Britain since 1807; however, the United States had not taken advantage of the intervening years to strengthen its military forces. At the time of the declaration of war, the Army had an actual strength of less than 7,000 men. In January, 1812, Congress had increased the authorized strength of the Army to 35,000, but little had been accomplished in obtaining volunteers to fill the paper authorization. At the same time, the British Army in Canada numbered less than 5,000 men.[18]

If the United States Congress had visualized the seriousness of the situation with Britain and initiated mandatory military service when it authorized an increase in the strength of the Army

---

[17]Emory Upton, The Military Policy of the United States, p. 95.
[18]Frederick L. Huidekoper, The Military Unpreparedness of the United States, p. 53.

in January, 1812, America could have been in a position to destroy the British in Canada at the beginning of the war. The conflict with France prevented sufficient British reinforcement to insure victory on the American continent.

The United States experienced unbelievable difficulty in mobilizing the militia. The New England states opposed the war with Great Britain, and the states of Connecticut and Massachusetts firmly rejected the authority of the United States to mobilize the militia. The intent of the mobilization was to replace the regular forces in the states with the militia. The regular forces, which had been guarding the seacoast, were scheduled to be sent north to participate in the invasion of Canada. The states based their objections upon the provision that the militia could be used to carry out the laws of the nation, subdue an insurrection, and repel an invasion. None of these conditions existed within the states concerned, and the militia was not turned out.[19]

Fortunately for the United States, Great Britain was deeply involved in the Peninsular War at the time of the War of 1812. This kept the majority of the small, highly trained British Army in Europe throughout the greater part of the war in America. The British Navy was successful in dominating the sea lanes and blockading commercial shipping off the eastern coast of the United States; however, the United States Navy was the one bright spot in the American military actions in the war. Although outnumbered and

----

[19]Ibid., p. 53.

outgunned, the United States Navy gave a fine performance and engaged the British Navy successfully on Lake Erie and Lake Champlain. The defeats suffered by the British Navy in the latter two battles interrupted movement and support for the British Army, and the United States Army benefited from the American naval victories.[20]

The United States employed over 500,000 men in the armed forces at one time or other during the war. The greatest number of troops were used during 1814 when over 200,000 men were called up for duty. The United States seldom concentrated more than 3,000 troops at any one time or place to engage the British Army. This permitted the British, who at no time counted over 17,000 men, to keep the American Army fully occupied. The United States, a comparatively new nation, lacked enthusiastic leadership and popular support throughout the war. The New England states openly opposed the war, and certain states continued commercial trade with the British. There was a dearth of military leaders capable of providing the command and inspiration needed to cope with the small but professional British Army. The American Army had superiority in numbers throughout the entire war; however, the commanders were unable to mass sufficient troops to make a successful attack against the smaller British force.[21]

------

[20]Upton, op. cit., pp. 107-120, 123-133, 138-139.
[21]Burt, op. cit., pp. 317-344.

FOREIGN DIPLOMACY

The diplomatic experience of the United States had been limited prior to the War of 1812. The foreign policy guidance of the nation had been established by George Washington in his farewell address when he stated:

> The Great rule of conduct for us, in regard to foreign nations, is, in extending our commercial relations, to have with them as little political connection as possible. So far as we have already formed engagements, let them be fulfilled with perfect good faith. . . . Here let us stop.

> Europe has a set of primary interests, which to us have none, or a very remote relation. Hence she must be engaged in frequent controversies, the causes of which are essentially foreign to our concerns. Hence, therefore, it must be unwise in us to implicate ourselves by artificial ties, in the ordinary combinations and collisions of her friendships, or enmities.[22]

With the exception of various trade agreements which the United States made with the European nations, the profound counsel of Washington had been followed. The foreign policy of the United States had developed into neutrality, but had not isolated the nation from commercial intercourse with the nations of the world. In fact, as noted previously, the wars raging in Europe prior to the War of 1812 had bolstered the economy of the United States.

The diplomacy of the United States consisted of a continuous effort to negotiate a peace with the British throughout the entire period of the war. Great Britain eliminated the primary diplomatic

---

[22]George Washington, The Farewell Address, pp. 37-38.

obstacle prior to the beginning of the war when the government revoked the Orders in Council. The British hoped that this would result in an early peace, but the United States continued to demand that Great Britain abandon the practice of impressing American sailors on the high seas. The British refuted this demand, and extinguished the flame of hope for an early peace.[23]

In March, 1813, Russia offered to mediate the differences between Great Britain and the United States. The United States immediately accepted the offer, and designated and dispatched peace commissioners to Russia. Upon arrival in Russia the Chancellor of Russia informed them that Great Britain had rejected the Russian proposal of mediation. In November, 1813, Great Britain suggested that an attempt be made to conclude the war by direct negotiation, and the United States accepted this proposal in January, 1814. Ghent, then a part of United Netherlands, was selected as the location for the peace conference.[24]

Both nations approached the conference table as victors of the war, which was a ridiculous position for the conferees of either nation to take. Throughout the negotiations their positions were dependent upon the information concerning the progress of the war received from America and the political developments taking place on the European continent. The American delegation was unable to bargain from a position of strength when news of the burning of

---

[23]Albert Z. Carr, The Coming of War, p. 331.
[24]Burt, op. cit., pp. 347-348.

Washington reached Europe. Likewise, when the news arrived telling of the great American victory over the British Navy on Lake Champlain, the British conferees found themselves on the defensive.[25]

Finally, on Christmas Eve, 1814, the Articles of the Treaty of Ghent were agreed upon by the representatives of both nations. The treaty provided little more than the rules under which the war was to end. There was no mention of the conditions which stimulated the war. Interference with neutral shipping, impressment of sailors, and freedom of the seas were conspicuous by their omission. Provision was made for the return of territory to the nation having possession at the beginning of the war, and a system was established whereby designated commissioners of both nations determined the boundaries between Canada and the United States. In short, after the War of 1812 ended, the status quo ante bellum was restored.[26]

SUMMARY

In the War of 1812 the United States resorted to the use of armed force when peaceful negotiations failed to resolve the differences which had arisen with Great Britain over the freedom of the seas. Consideration was not given by the government to the weak condition of the American military forces, and little effort was put forth by Congress to improve the status of the Army or Navy prior to declaration of war. Unsatisfactory national control over

---

[25]Mahan, op. cit., Vol. 2, pp. 415-432.
[26]U.S. Treaties, etc., Vol. 2, Treaty of Ghent, pp. 574-584.

the mobilization of the militia was disastrous, and the limited success in military operations against smaller British forces emphasized the military deficiencies of the United States.

The military did not contribute directly to the success of the United States diplomacy at Ghent; however, the limited successes of the American forces provided bargaining points for the diplomats to employ in their discussions with the British representatives.

CHAPTER 3

SPANISH AMERICAN WAR

Armed intervention in the Cuban revolution in 1898 thrust the United States into the world power arena. Neutralism was forgotten as the expansionists preached of larger navies, importance of world power, need for foreign possessions, and the economic advantage of more overseas markets. The Spanish American War can be considered the turning point in American history which led the United States on the way to imperialism.[1]

CUBAN INSURRECTION, 1868-1878

In 1825 the King of Spain, having lost all colonies in the new world except Cuba and Porto Rico (Puerto Rico), issued instructions to the Captain-General in Cuba which literally placed the island under martial law. The instructions established the Captain-General as a virtual dictator, and all rights of the individual were negated. Between 1825 and 1868 several attempts were made by native Cubans and Cuban sympathizers to invade the island. These invasions failed because of insufficient popular support and betrayals by informers.[2]

By 1868, Queen Isabella II of Spain was exiled by a reform party which objected to the immorality of her rule. This weakened

---

[1]Foster R. Dulles, America's Rise to World Power, 1898-1954, p. 40.

[2]Walter Millis, The Martial Spirit, pp. 10-13.

the government of Spain, and several years elapsed before the nation established a stable government. The rebels in Cuba seized this opportunity to revolt openly against the intolerable Spanish controls; and in October, 1868, declared independence from Spain. A constitution was prepared, an army of 15,000 poorly equipped irregulars was organized, and a war of insurgency was launched against the Spanish. The war lasted for ten years, and consisted of guerrilla tactics by the Cubans against the more formal military tactics of the Spanish. The geography of the island favored the tactics of the insurgents; however, both forces were guilty of committing atrocities during the conduct of the war.[3]

The Ten Years War ended in February, 1878. The Pact of El Zanjon, agreed to by the insurgents and the Spanish, provided the following: freedom for all who had taken part in the war on the side of the rebels, freedom to all slaves who had fought in the war, and transportation for any of the insurgents who desired to leave Cuba. Although the insurgents expected conditions to be improved greatly subsequent to 1878, it was apparent that the Spanish leaders on the island complied only with the reforms favorable to Spain.[4]

Certain Americans looked upon the insurrection in Cuba as an opportunity for the United States to exert its influence in the Caribbean. The memory of the Civil War, fresh in the minds of many

---

[3]Charles Morris, The War With Spain, pp. 38-44.
[4]Henry Cabot Lodge, The War With Spain, pp. 11-12.

17

people in the North and South, made involvement in another war unpopular. Nevertheless, President Grant decided to recognize the new Cuban republic, and in 1869 placed his signature on a document taking cognizance of the belligerency in Cuba. Fortunately for the United States, Secretary of State Fish had the foresight to withhold this document from publication; and in June, 1870, he persuaded President Grant to send a message to Congress explaining that the Cuban insurrection did not justify recognition as a belligerency.[5] Pertinent portions of the text of his message are quoted:

> In my annual message to Congress, at the beginning of its present session, I referred to the contest which had then for more than a year existed in the Island of Cuba between a portion of its inhabitants and the Government of Spain, and the feelings and sympathies of the people and Government of the United States for the people of Cuba, as for all peoples struggling for liberty and self-government, and said that 'the contest has at no time assumed the conditions which amount to war, in the sense of international law, or which would show the existence of a de facto political organization of the insurgents sufficient to justify a recognition of belligerency.'
>
> During the six months which have passed since the date of that message, the condition of the insurgents has not improved; and the insurrection itself, although not subdued, exhibits no signs of advance, but seems to be confined to an irregular system of hostilities, carried on by small and illy-armed bands of men, roaming, without concentration, through the woods and sparsely populated regions of the island, attacking from ambush convoys and small bands of troops, burning plantations and the estates of those not sympathizing with their cause.
>
> *   *   *   *   *
>
> In the uncertainty that hangs around the entire insurrection there is no palpable evidence of an election, of any delegated authority, or of any Government outside the limits of the camps occupied from day to

---

[5]Walter Millis, Arms and Men, p. 132.

day by the roving companies of insurgent troops. There
is no commerce; no trade, either internal or foreign; no
manufactures.

* * * * *

If it be war between Spain and Cuba, and be so recognized, it is our duty to provide for the consequences
which may ensue in the embarrassment to our commerce
and the interference with our revenue.

If belligerency be recognized, the commercial marine of
the United States becomes liable to search and to seizure by the commissioned cruisers of both parties . . .
they become subject to the adjudication of prize courts.

* * * * *

. . . Solemn protests have been made against every
infraction of the rights either of individual citizens
of the United States or the rights of our flag upon
the high seas, and all proper steps have been taken
and are being pressed for the proper reparation of
every indignity complained of.[6]

The relationship between Spain and the United States was strained

when a Spanish gunboat captured the American-registered ship

Virginius. This ship was suspected of gun-running and carrying

cargo to the insurgents in Cuba. At the time of capture the

Virginius was carrying arms and passengers apparently destined for

Cuba. Some fifty members of the crew and passengers were killed

indiscriminately by the Spanish before diplomatic protests and the

arrival of a British ship at the scene brought an end to the

massacre. Aware of the disreputable record of the ship, the United

States made a tongue-in-cheek protest of the incident to Spain

through diplomatic channels. Spain proved that the ship was

---

[6]Francis Wharton, ed., A Digest of International Law of the
United States, Vol. I, pp. 384-389.

fraudulently registered as a United States ship, but agreed to pay damages to the families of the men who had been killed. The insurgent activity continued in Cuba and became increasingly more objectionable to the United States. It was necessary to establish patrols along the eastern and southern coasts of the United States to prevent Cuban sympathizers from shipping goods and men to Cuba from the United States. Finally, in the fall of 1875, Secretary of State Fish notified Spain that, unless some effort was made to reconcile the aims of the opposing forces in Cuba, it might be necessary for other governments to intervene. At this time Spain was undergoing another governmental upheaval, and little progress in terminating the war was expected or accomplished. The war continued, and finally an unsatisfactory peace agreement ended the war in 1878.[7]

Serious confrontation between Spain and the United States over the insurgency in Cuba was averted by diplomatic means throughout the ten year period of the war. Why was this means unsuccessful twenty years later, when once again rebel insurrection against Spain ravaged the island?

CHANGING AMERICAN THINKING

Thirty years passed between the Civil War and the Spanish American War. The horrors of war had been forgotten by the American people, a new generation was making its presence felt, the scare of

---

[7]Millis, The Martial Spirit, pp. 14-16.

a depression in 1893 had passed, and nationalism swept across the country like a tidal wave. When the insurrection in Cuba ignited again in 1895, the insurgents adopted a scorched earth policy which damaged American properties and interests as well as those of the Spanish. This action eventually forced General Weyler, the Spanish Captain-General of Cuba, to establish concentration camps for civilians to prevent their aiding and abetting the insurgents. The majority of the inhabitants of these camps were women and children; and, due to food shortage and pathological conditions, many innocent people perished from starvation and disease.[8]

American citizens were among those who were imprisoned, and public indignation in the United States was widespread. In fairness to the Spanish, it must be noted that some of the American citizens were in sympathy with the insurgents, and many of these were naturalized American citizens with Cuban parentage.[9]

William Randolph Hearst purchased a defunct newspaper, the New York Journal, in 1895, and immediately set out to attain the leadership in American journalism held by Joseph Pulitzer and his New York World. The desire of these men to dominate the news field was so great that their responsibility for reporting accurate news and true facts was forgotten. Both newspapers exaggerated conditions in Cuba to such an extent that many of the news releases were pure fabrication on the part of the reporters and editors. Although

---

[8]Morris, op. cit., pp. 77, 92-96.
[9]Ibid., p. 97.

21

this yellow journalism influenced the state of mind of the public, other factors contributed to molding public opinion into a desire for intervention in Cuba.[10]

President Cleveland, under great pressure from the press, the people of the nation, and members of the Congress to intervene in the Cuban insurrection, held firmly to his conviction that the United States should not recognize the insurgents in Cuba. At the outbreak of the rebellion he issued a proclamation which established the neutrality of the United States. He enforced neutrality, and established patrols to prevent the operation of gun-runners and filibusters in support of the insurrection. The American patrols established effective blockades to prevent shipping from leaving the shores of the United States, but the Spanish failed in preventing cargo shipments from landing in Cuba once they evaded the American patrols. It was understood by both Spain and the United States that the insurrection would have failed without the support of the Cuban sympathizers in America.[11]

Three incidents happened in succession in the early part of 1898 and provided the _finale_ to the change in the American thinking concerning involvement in the Cuban insurrection. The Spanish Minister in Washington, Don Enrique Dupuy de Lome, wrote a letter containing derogatory comments about President McKinley. The letter fell into the hands of the Cuban insurgents who arranged for its

---

[10]L. Ethan Ellis, _A Short History of American Diplomacy_, p. 268.
[11]Allan Nevins, _Grover Cleveland, A Study in Courage_, p. 714.

publication by the Cuban Junta in New York. Next, the United States battleship Maine was destroyed in Havana by a mysterious explosion which cost the lives of two officers and two hundred and sixty-four members of the crew. Finally, Senator Proctor, from Vermont, reported to the Senate on his recent visit to Cuba, and he described the unbelievable misery of the horrible living conditions.[12]

The public of the United States was emotional over conditions in Cuba, and war with Spain was inevitable.

DIPLOMACY?

When President McKinley took office in March, 1897, sympathy for the Cuban insurrection had declined somewhat in the United States. President McKinley believed substantially the same as his predecessor concerning the involvement of the United States in the Cuban rebellion; however, the attitude of the people described above was quite different from that which President Cleveland faced prior to leaving office. In addition, President McKinley did not have a strong Secretary of State comparable to Hamilton Fish, Secretary under Grant; or Richard Olney, Secretary under Cleveland.[13]

Charles S. Olcott, in his book The Life of William McKinley, identified the basic problem which faced the new President when he wrote:

---

[12]Charles S. Olcott, The Life of William McKinley, Vol. 2, pp. 8-15.

[13]James T. Adams, The Epic of America, pp. 334-335.

The Cuban question, at the beginning of the McKinley Administration presented a three-fold aspect: (1) The relief of the suffering; (2) the question of belligerency or the recognition of independence; and (3) the possibility of intervention to end the war.[14]

The problem was little different when Cleveland had been in office, but McKinley was opposed by members of his own party who were anxious for the United States to intervene in the Spanish-Cuban conflagration. Henry Cabot Lodge indicated the sentiment of some of the leaders in a letter to Theodore Roosevelt on May 24, 1898, when he stated: "Porto Rico is not forgotten and we mean to have it. Unless I am utterly and profoundly mistaken the Administration is now fully committed to the large policy that we both desire."[15] The United States had declared war upon Spain a month before this letter was written; however, it exemplifies the pressure under which the President was working.

After many weeks of fruitless negotiation, the Minister to Spain, Mr. Woodford, was instructed on March 27, 1898, to query the Spanish government regarding the following: establishment of an Armistice until October 1, during which time negotiations would be implemented between Cuban insurgents and Spain; revocation of the orders effecting concentration of the Cubans in cities and concentration camps; and, in event peace could not be established by October 1, the President of the United States would intervene as

---

[14]Olcott, op. cit., Vol. I, p. 395.
[15]Henry Cabot Lodge, ed., Selections from the Correspondence of Theodore Roosevelt and Henry Cabot Lodge, Vol. I, pp. 299-300.

an arbiter between the insurgents and Spain. It was impossible
for the Spanish government to accept these provisions without losing
face in the European community and exposing the nation to possible
revolution.[16]

Spain was in no position, however, to become involved in a
war with the United States; and by the 9th of April the Spanish
Governor in Cuba was instructed to grant an armistice for as long
a period as he might determine necessary and to revoke the concentration orders. This action partially satisfied the official
demands of the United States, but was insufficient to satisfy the
bellicose elements of the nation. The slow turning of the diplomatic
wheel exasperated the Americans, and the demand for action by the
public and the public servants eventually brought about Presidential
approval of a condition of war between the United States and Spain.
This approval was given on April 25, 1898, retroactive to April 21.[17]

Diplomacy failed in preventing a confrontation over the freedom
of Cuba and the inhuman treatment of the people of Cuba, but
President McKinley worked diligently to direct the ship of negotiation
in the direction of peaceful settlement. He recognized the difficult
position of the Spanish government; however, it appeared that the
promises made by Spain constituted another effort to delay the final
decision of war.

---

[16]Millis, The Martial Spirit, pp. 129-130.
[17]Lodge, The War With Spain, p. 44.

WAR AND RESULTS

The Spanish American War launched the United States into the middle of world affairs as a world power, but the unpreparedness of the American military establishment for employment in the war was demonstrated almost immediately. The United States Army was the least prepared of the two services, and the success it achieved in Cuba was more a result of ineptness on the part of the Spanish Army than efficiency on the part of the US Army.

Tension had existed between the United States and Spain for thirty years over the deplorable conditions in Cuba; nevertheless, at the time of the outbreak of war, the United States had not prepared plans for operations on the island. In fact, no plans existed to cover the joint operations of the Army and Navy in an amphibious situation, and there was no provision for a properly staffed command organization to control the forces of both services in the target area.[18]

Theodore Roosevelt, in a letter to Henry Cabot Lodge on June 10, 1898, described some of the difficulties encountered by units of the US Army as it prepared to embark for Cuba.

> No words can describe to you the confusion and lack of
> system and the general mismanagement of affairs here;
> a good deal of it is inevitable accompaniment of a
> sudden war where people have resolutely refused to make
> the needed preparations, but a good deal could be
> avoided. . . . When we unloaded our regiment at Tampa
> we had to go 24 hours without food and not a human

---

[18]US Army, Reserve Officers Training Corps Manual 145-20, pp. 297-300 (referred to hereafter as ROTCM 145-20).

> being met us to show us our camp or tell us anything
> about what we were to do. . . . We had to hunt all
> over the dock among ten thousand people before, by
> chance we ran across first one and then the other,
> and each regiment had to seize its transport and hold
> it against all comers; nothing but the most vigorous,
> and rather lawless, work got us our transport.[19]

Despite the small size of the Regular Army (28,000 at the beginning of the war), the nonexistence of a mobilization plan, the inadequate and obsolete equipment, the lack of competent leaders, and the poorly trained reserve force, the US Army invaded the island of Cuba, and defeated the superior numbers of the Spanish Army. It then moved to Puerto Rico and secured that island for the United States with little opposition.[20]

The US Navy was far better prepared than the US Army for the war with Spain. The importance of sea power, emphasized by Captain Mahan for a number of years, was recognized by the nation. The Navy had been modernizing and constructing new ships during the previous ten years. At the beginning of the war Commodore Dewey was located at Hong Kong ready for action against the Spanish fleet which was located at Manila in the Philippines. This was not accidental. Theodore Roosevelt, _acting_ in the capacity of Secretary of Navy, directed Dewey to take station at Hong Kong and be prepared to sail against the Spanish fleet in Manila in the event war developed between the United States and Spain.[21]

---

[19]Lodge, Selections from the Correspondence of Theodore Roosevelt and Henry Cabot Lodge, Vol. I, pp. 303-304.

[20]ROTCM 145-20, p. 308.

[21]Millis, The Martial Spirit, p. 112.

The US Navy met success in all of its endeavors during the war. Although the requirement to protect the cities along the eastern coast of the United States from possible attack by the Spanish Navy reduced the naval capability, the combat efficiency of the fleet was not seriously affected. The absence of an overall commander for the Army and Navy at Santiago, Cuba, might have been grievous to the Navy; however, the action taken by Admiral Cervera to escape Santiago Bay with the Spanish fleet, resulting in the complete destruction of his armada, eliminated the cause for disagreement between the commanders of the US Navy and US Army.[22]

Commodore Dewey completely destroyed the Spanish fleet located at Manila on May 1, 1898, and within a short time had silenced the artillery batteries which protected the harbor city. Although Dewey had little difficulty in overcoming the Spanish fleet, he was unable to capture Manila, and was forced to request US Army ground forces to secure the city. Upon the arrival of the Army forces in July, 1898, the Spanish surrendered the city, and the armistice was signed on August 14.[23]

The Peace Protocol was agreed upon by Spain and the United States on August 12, 1898, two days before the armistice in Manila; and the Spanish American War was terminated. The Protocol gave Cuba, Puerto Rico and one of the Ladrones, which was to be selected at a later date, to the United States; and authorized the United

---

[22]ROTCM 145-20, pp. 300-301, 307-309.
[23]Ibid., pp. 300-301, 309-310.

States to maintain its position in the Philippine Islands until the final disposition of the islands was determined.[24]

As the war ended the United States awakened to find that it was a colonial power with possessions spread halfway around the world. The nation had flexed its muscles at an old European power, and had demonstrated to the world that the young man of the western hemisphere had reached maturity. The people were pleased with the results of the war, but few realized that expansion into the world outside the limits of continental United States involved far more than the annexation of territory. Expansion contained the responsibility for the people who inhabited the newly acquired possessions, and the problems which formerly troubled Spain now confronted the United States. An insurrection erupted in the Philippine Islands, and it became apparent that the natives of the islands had no more desire to be governed by the Americans than by the Spanish. More American lives were lost in the military operations against the rebels in the Philippine Islands than were lost in the Spanish American War.[25]

As a world power, the United States found that many problems required immediate resolution and that the entrance into imperialism established a basis for future foreign entanglements in world politics. The status of Cuba, Hawaii, Guam, and the Philippine Islands was in question. How were these possessions to be governed? Were the natives to be citizens of the United States, or were they subjects?

---

[24]Lodge, The War With Spain, pp. 259-261.
[25]ROTCM 145-20, pp. 310-311.

SUMMARY

The Spanish American War permitted full expression of the desires of the American people to make the power of the United States recognized in the world. It revealed modern, forward looking personalities in the government who visualized the future destiny of the nation. On the somber side of the war, inefficiency and ineptness in some areas of the government were revealed, and the military departments were not above criticism.

It was demonstrated clearly that a strong, efficient Navy was required to insure the security of the United States. Revitalization of the Army and the requirement for a sealift capability to any area in the world to protect American interests was recognized. The confusion which existed during the early stages of the Cuban campaign emphasized the need for a military staff to supervise military matters in peacetime and to insure military readiness in event of war.

Assistant Secretary of Navy Theodore Roosevelt, sometimes accused of impulsiveness and bellicosity, recognized the importance of the military in foreign affairs; and his actions which employed the fleet of Commodore Dewey in the Pacific utilized a military force in direct support of diplomatic action.

CHAPTER 4

THE TWO WORLD WARS

> I would like first to say a word about the total result
> of these two world wars in Europe. These wars were
> fought at the price of some tens of millions of lives,
> of untold physical destruction, of the destruction of
> the balance of forces on the Continent . . . at the
> price of rendering western Europe dangerously, perhaps
> fatefully, vulnerable to Soviet power. Both wars were
> fought, really, with the view to changing Germany:
> to correct her behavior, to making the Germans some-
> thing different from what they were. Yet, today, if
> one were offered the chance of having back again the
> Germany of 1913 . . . a Germany run by conservative
> but relatively moderate people, no Nazis and no Com-
> munists, a vigorous Germany, united and unoccupied,
> full of energy and confidence, able to play a part
> again in the balancing-off of Russian power in Europe
> . . . well, there would be objections to it from many
> quarters, and it wouldn't make everybody happy; but in
> many ways it wouldn't sound so bad, in comparison with
> our problems of today.[1]

Reading the above statement by Mr. George F. Kennan, from his book

American Diplomacy, 1900-1950, tends to infect one with nostalgia.

The thought of the "good old days" enters the mind, and the dream

of total peace in the world begins anew. The connection between

these two wars is alluded to; and the dissatisfaction of man in

the results of the wars is evident in the ideal proposed in retro-

spect, the suggestion that the world would be a better place in

which to live, if the wars had not taken place. The facts of

reality cannot be denied; the wars did take place, and the involve-

_ment of the United States in the two wars resulted from similar causes.

---

[1]George F. Kennan, American Diplomacy, 1900-1950, pp. 56-57.

31

NEUTRALITY

In Webster's Dictionary neutrality is defined as:

The state or condition of being neutral or of being
unengaged in disputes or contests between others;
the state of taking no part on either side; in international law, that condition of a nation or state in
which it does not take part directly or indirectly
in a war between other states.[2]

The United States professed neutrality in the initial stages of both

World War I and World War II. The belligerent nations, in need of

equipment and supplies to continue successfully the war, were

interested in trading with the United States. Industry in the

United States was in need of additional markets, and the opportunity

for a neutral to profit from the misfortunes of the warring nations

could not be ignored. As in the War of 1812, the opportunity for

economic gain and the danger of involvement in war went hand in

hand, with expanding trade resulting in considerable controversy

between the bellicose nations and the United States.[3]

In the first World War the British Navy was in position to

prevent Germany from obtaining supplies and munitions from the

United States. The German government objected and claimed that

the United States was violating neutrality by providing the supplies

to Great Britain when Germany was unable to obtain an equal amount.

The primary argument between Germany and the United States developed

over the age-old question of the freedom of the seas. Germany

---

[2]Harold Whitehall, ed., Webster's New Twentieth Century Dictionary, p. 1130. (Underlining added.)
[3]US Dept of State, Peace and War, pp. 483-486.

started mining the sea lanes and attacking shipping indiscriminately, and the British sowed mines in the North Sea in retaliation. In addition, the British implemented a system of blockades and black-lists which resulted in vast disruption of neutral shipping. The difference between the restrictions implemented by Great Britain and Germany revolved around the loss of life. The actions taken by the British placed a premium upon property, while the actions implemented by the Germans not only destroyed property but human life as well. This loss of American life was instrumental in turning the public opinion in the United States against Germany, and Great Britain became favored in the eyes of the majority of the American citizens. The return to unrestricted submarine warfare by the Germans, which negated the assurance given the United States on May 4, 1916, concerning the cessation of this type of attack, and the attempt by Germany to effect an alliance with Mexico against the United States prompted President Wilson to request a declaration of war against Germany.[4]

Between the two wars the American public, disillusioned by the results of World War I and the depression, exerted pressure on the government to restrict exportation of ammunition, arms, and any implement of war. The masses believed that the previous war had resulted from the distribution of military hardware by the United States to the European nations. Congress passed a joint resolution, known as the Neutrality Act of 1935, making the export of arms,

---

[4]War Memoirs of Robert Lansing, pp. 210-212.

ammunition, or implements of war illegal. The resolution further prohibited the transport of arms to belligerent nations on United States shipping and travel of United States citizens on ships of belligerent nations.[5]

In November, 1939, Congress enacted legislation to relax the embargo on arms, ammunition, and implements of war; and opposing nations were authorized to transport their cash-and-carry property from United States territory. The President was empowered to designate the limits of combat areas into which citizens or vessels of the United States could not enter.[6]

This was one of the actions which slowly moved the United States into alliance with Great Britain and the western nations. Winston Churchill, in his book Their Finest Hour, commented upon the transfer of United States destroyers to Great Britain in exchange for lease of certain bases in Newfoundland, the Bahamas, and Jamaica.

> The transfer to Great Britain of fifty American warships was a decidedly unneutral act by the United States. It would, according to all the standards of history, have justified the German Government in declaring war upon them. The President judged that there was no danger, and I felt there was no hope, of this simple solution of many difficulties. It was Hitler's interest and method to strike his opponents down one by one. The last thing he wished was to be drawn into war with the United States before he had finished with Britain. Nevertheless the transfer of destroyers to Britain in August, 1940, was an event which brought the United States definitely nearer to us and to the war, and it was the first of a long succession of increasingly unneutral

---

[5]US Dept of State, Peace and War, pp. 266-271.
[6]Ibid., pp. 494-506.

acts in the Atlantic which were of the utmost service to
us. It marked the passage of the United States from
being neutral to being nonbelligerent. Although Hitler
could not afford to resent it, all the world, as will
be seen, understood the significance of the gesture.[7]

Implementation of the destroyer deal with Great Britain invalidated
the neutrality of the United States. The American people, desirous
of remaining out of the European war, wanted to assist the victims
of aggression. This pushed the nation ever closer to the brink of
war. The granting of lend-lease, the armed escort of convoys, and
economic sanctions against Japan did not endear the United States
to Germany and Japan. The Axis powers had cause to consider the
United States an undeclared ally of Great Britain.

FAILURE OF TALKING DIPLOMACY

A similarity existed in the diplomacy of World War I and World
War II. On June 9, 1915, William Jennings Bryan resigned as
Secretary of State in President Wilson's Cabinet. His primary
reason for resigning this position was his objection to President
Wilson's policy in dealing with the German government concerning
the loss of American lives in the sinking of the Lusitania. Bryan
believed that American travel aboard belligerent ships carrying
contraband was not justified. He expressed this belief and sub-
mitted his resignation for he could no longer support the President.[8]

---

[7]Winston S. Churchill, The Second World War: Their Finest Hour,
p. 404.
[8]W. J. Bryan and M. B. Bryan, The Memoirs of William Jennings
Bryan, pp. 395-428.

Robert Lansing, Bryan's successor as Secretary of State,
prepared a memorandum outlining his concept of the foreign policy
to be pursued by the United States. Pertinent portions are quoted
below:

> I have come to the conclusiin that the German Government
> is utterly hostile to all nations with democratic insti-
> tutions because those who compose it see in democracy a
> menace to absolutism and the defeat of the German ambi-
> tion for world domination. Everywhere German agents are
> plotting and intriguing to accomplish the supreme purpose
> of their government.
>
> Only recently has the conviction come to me that demoe-
> racy throughout the world is threatened. Suspicions of
> the vaguest sort only a few months ago have been more
> and more confirmed. From many sources evidence has
> been coming until it would be folly to close one's eyes
> to it.

*   *   *   *   *

> The remedy seems to me to be plain. It is that Germany
> must not be permitted to win this war or to break even,
> though to prevent it this country is forced to take an
> active part. This ultimate necessity must be constantly
> in our minds in all our controversies with the bellig-
> erents. American public opinion must be prepared for
> the time, which may come, when we will have to cast
> aside our neutrality and become one of the champions of
> democracy.[9]

This direct approach to support for Great Britain and her allies

by the Secretary of State predicted the failure of American neu-

trality. The person directly responsible for American diplomacy

possessed a preconceived opinion that one of the belligerents was

right and the other wrong. Thus, no matter what took place, the

final decision could not be objective in relation to each state.

---

[9]War Memoirs of Robert Lansing, pp. 19-21.

The sentiments of the leaders of the United States just prior to World War II paralleled those of the leaders in World War I.

In his message to Congress on January 4, 1939, President Roosevelt indicated that there were lawless nations in the world which were carrying out acts of aggression against sister nations. He emphasized that the United States need not intervene but declared that any action taken or not taken should in no way assist the aggressor governments.[10]

Some nine months prior to this message to Congress, Secretary of State Cordell Hull in a speech in Washington had stated: "Isolation is not a means to security; it is a fruitful source of insecurity." This was an early warning to the people of the United States that indifference to world strife would not keep the United States free from war.[11]

The leaders in the United States were aware of the potential trouble lurking in the shadows of the world. President Roosevelt, early in 1938, proposed to the British government that the United States sponsor a world conference to discuss differences in a cordial environment. Prime Minister Chamberlain disagreed with the proposal. He feared that the leaders of the totalitarian states would disregard the offer and use it as an excuse for breaking diplomatic relations with Great Britain.[12]

---

[10]US Dept of State, Peace and War, pp. 447-450.
[11]Ibid., p. 418.
[12]Winston S. Churchill, The Second World War: The Gathering Storm, pp. 251-254.

As indicated in the preceding comments on neutrality, the United States moved toward active participation in World War II against Germany and the Axis powers. The US Navy became involved in action in the North Atlantic Ocean. The US Army moved units to Iceland to establish an outpost and prevent Germany from securing the island. On September 11, 1941, President Roosevelt announced the diplomatic position of the United States. He stated:

> Normal practices of diplomacy--note writing--are of no possible use in dealing with international outlaws who sink our ships and kill our citizens.
>
> One peaceful nation after another has met disaster because each refused to look the Nazi danger squarely in the eye until it actually had them by the throat.
>
> The United States will not make that fatal mistake.
>
> *   *   *   *   *
>
> Upon our naval and air patrol--now operating in large number over the vast expanse of the Atlantic Ocean-- falls the duty of maintaining the American policy of freedom of the seas--now. That means, very simply and clearly, that our patrolling vessels and planes will protect all merchant ships--not only American ships but ships of any flag--engaged in commerce of our defensive waters. They will protect them from submarines; they will protect them from surface raiders.[13]

This declaration admitted the failure of talking diplomacy, and emphasized the need for military forces to protect the interests of the nation.

---

[13]US Dept of State, Peace and War, pp. 742-743.

THE WARS

The details of the American military participation in World War I and World War II have provided the source material for many volumes since 1917. A comparison of the two wars reveals that the role of the United States was of greater importance in World War II than in World War I.

The United States cannot claim that the military forces provided won the First World War. Military experience was extremely limited, and, at the time of the Armistice, American forces had not yet reached their programed strength. The industrial resources of the United States, plus the military forces employed in Europe and on the sea, contributed greatly to the Allied victory. The momentum of American mobilization was building rapidly at the termination of the war.[14]

The First World War provided experience for the professional military of the United States. The US Army received valuable training in large-scale operations in an environment far from American shores, the US Navy gained experience in escorting large surface convoys, all forces received extensive experience in logistics and staff procedures, and exposure to the modern weapons in the war brought about new doctrine and techniques of warfare.[15]

---

[14]US Army, Reserve Officers Training Corps Manual, 145-20, pp. 338-340 (referred to hereafter as ROTCM 145-20).
[15]Ibid., pp. 334-335, 340-343.

Following World War I the United States failed to ratify the
Treaty of Versailles, which provided for participation in the League
of Nations sponsored by President Wilson. The United States remained
at war with Germany until 1921 when a separate peace treaty was
signed.[16]

The National Defense Act of 1920 provided for an Army of nearly
300,000 officers and men, and established the National Guard and
the Organized Reserves as civilian components of the Army. The
professional military man believed that a sound program had been
established for the military; however, the authorized strength of
the Army had been reduced to 137,000 officers and men by 1922. By
1933, the Army of the United States was 17th in strength among the
nations of the world.[17]

The withdrawal of the United States from world affairs was so
complete that the military was not concerned itself with the national
interests of the times. General Eisenhower expressed the attitude
prevalent among the military in his book, Crusade in Europe.

> In early 1940, however, the United States Army mirrored
> the attitudes of the American people, as is the case
> today and as it was a century ago. The mass of officers
> and men lacked any sense of urgency. Athletics, recre-
> ation, and entertainment took precedence in most units
> over serious training. Some of the officers, in the
> long years of peace, had worn for themselves deep ruts
> of professional routine within which they were sheltered
> from vexing new ideas and troublesome problems. Others,
> bogged down in one grade for many years because seniority
> was the basis for promotion, had abandoned all hope of
> progress. Possibly many of them, and many of the troops
> too, felt that the infantryman's day had passed.

---

[16] Ibid., p. 362.
[17] Ibid., pp. 363-367.

* * * * *

> The greatest obstacle was psychological--complacency still
> persisted! Even the fall of France in May 1940 failed
> to awaken us--and by 'us' I mean many professional sol-
> diers as well as others--to a full realization of danger.
> The commanding general of one United States division, an
> officer of long service and high standing, offered to
> bet, on the day of the French armistice, that England
> would not last six weeks longer--and he proposed the
> wager much as he would have bet on rain or shine for
> the morrow. It did not occur to him to think of Britain
> as the sole remaining belligerent standing between us
> and the starkest danger. His attitude was typical of
> soldiers and civilians alike. Happily there were numerous
> exceptions whose devoted efforts accomplished more than
> seemed possible.[18]

Although the armed forces of the United States were not fully

modernized at the beginning of the Second World War, the American

military machine developed into the greatest fighting organization

known to the world. Priority of operations was given to the

European theater of war, and the American forces in the Pacific

were supported to the extent necessary to insure survival. The

coalition of the United States and Great Britain in the western

part of Europe and North Africa, together with the operations of

the Russian forces in eastern Europe, resulted in the defeat of the

Axis powers. The power displayed by the United States, both mili-

tary and industrial, must be credited with turning the tide of

battle in favor of the Allies.[19]

Four months after the termination of the war in Europe General

MacArthur accepted the surrender of the Japanese. Employment of

---

[18]Dwight D. Eisenhower, Crusade in Europe, pp. 7-8.
[19]Winston S. Churchill, The Second World War: The Grand
Alliance, pp. 699-711.

atomic bombs on Hiroshima and Nagasaki on 6 and 9 August brought about a request for peace from Japan, and the war in the Pacific was officially concluded with the signing of the surrender documents aboard the USS Missouri on September 2, 1945.[20]

In December, 1941, the power of the United States military forces was almost negligible, a portion of the Navy had been destroyed at Pearl Harbor, and the ground forces had been defeated in all operations. In less than four years the US Army and the US Navy mobilized and made the United States a world power. Would this position of leadership be accepted and the military power be used to enforce peace?

SUMMARY

The two world wars thrust the United States directly into world leadership. Following World War I the nation refused to accept the responsibility placed upon it by the world, and hereditary isolation once again infected the Americans. They remembered the horrors of the war, but the grim reality that a German victory would have made the Atlantic coast America's first line of defense was forgotten. Neutrality laws were passed by Congress during the 1930's in an attempt to prevent legally any activity which might result in the United States participation in hostilities in the world. As the power of Germany and the Axis increased, the buffer nations of Great Britain and France provided the United States with time to gird itself for the second war in the same generation.

---

[20]ROTCM 145-20, pp. 441-443.

America provided much of the force which defeated the Axis powers in the Second World War, and at the end of the war the nation faced staggering commitments to preserve peace throughout the world. The powerful military machine could be used to make the nation imperialistic, alliances could be established to stabilize the balance of power, or collective security could be promoted through organized internationalism. The United States had a second chance, and the mistakes of World War I could not be repeated.

CHAPTER 5

MILITARY DIPLOMACY

Prior to the termination of World War II, action was taken to
establish an international organization to preclude future wars.
It was the fervent hope of the American people that such an organization might succeed where the League of Nations had failed.
Visions of a lasting peace once more infiltrated the dreams of the
public. The brief discussion which follows will touch on incidents
which have brightened, blurred, or destroyed the vision of peace
since World War II.

THE UNITED NATIONS

The importance of the United States in world affairs was
demonstrated by its leadership in the establishment of the United
Nations. The part the United States played in the organization
involved forsaking a long history of isolationism. One means of
insuring peace was established by Article 43 of the Charter of the
United Nations, which provided for the creation of an international
military force to operate under the control of the Security Council.
The eventual success of such a provision was questionable from the
start.[1]

---

[1]United Nations, Office of Public Information, Charter of the
United Nations and Statute of the International Court of Justice,
pp. 23-24.

Prime Minister Churchill seemed to have a premonition concerning the desire of the Soviet Union to participate in such a cooperative arrangement when he wrote to President Truman in May, 1945.

> I am profoundly concerned about the European situation.
> . . . Anyone can see that in a very short space of
> time our armed power on the Continent will have vanished,
> except for moderate forces to hold down Germany. Mean-
> while what is to happen about Russia? I have always
> worked for friendship with Russia, but, like you, I
> feel deep anxiety because of their misinterpretation
> of the Yalta decisions, their attitude towards Poland,
> their overwhelming influence in the Balkans. . . .
> What will be the position in a year or two, when the
> British and American Armies have melted and the French
> has not yet formed on any major scale, when we may have
> a handful of divisions, mostly French, and when Russia
> may choose to keep two or three hundred on active
> service?[2]

Failure to establish an international military force in the United Nations made it inevitable that regional collective agreements would arise from the provisions of Articles 51 and 52 of the United Nations Charter. The United States participated in collective agreements to assist in the maintenance of peace. The North Atlantic Treaty Organization is an example of such an agreement.[3]

On March 12, 1947, President Truman addressed both Houses of Congress, and emphasized the threat of the Soviet Union in the Mediterranean area. The President specifically asked for approval to provide economic and military aid to Greece and Turkey because of the direct pressures being placed on these nations by the Soviets. President Truman stated:

---

[2]Winston S. Churchill, The Second World War; Triumph and Tragedy, pp. 572-573.
[3]United Nations, op. cit., pp. 27-29.

I believe that it must be the policy of the United
States to support free peoples who are resisting
attempted subjugation by armed minorities or by outside pressures. . . . The seeds of totalitarian
regimes are nurtured by misery and want. They spread
and grow in the evil soil of poverty and strife. They
reach their full growth when the hope of a people for
a better life has died. . . . We must keep that hope
alive. The free people of the world look to us for
support in maintaining their freedoms.[4]

This speech confirmed the willingness of the United States to
accept world responsibilities. It announced the intentions of the
United States to contain the expansion of communism and opened the
door to the restoration of the prostrate European economy.[5]

NORTH ATLANTIC TREATY ORGANIZATION

The Berlin Blockade in 1948-1949 impressed upon many of the
Europeans the need for closer military ties between the nations of
the west. From this came the discussions which eventually resulted
in the formation of NATO. The United States had demonstrated its
sincerity in opposing communism in Europe by the establishment of
the Berlin Airlift, and the success of this action demonstrated
the will of the Americans to resist Communist aggression.[6]

The North Atlantic Treaty, signed at Washington, D.C., on
April 4, 1949, banded together states to insure the continuance of
peace through collective strength. The North Atlantic Treaty Organization is a military establishment with a peaceful goal. The member

---

[4]Harry S. Truman, Memoirs: Years of Trial and Hope, pp. 105-106.
[5]Ibid., pp. 110-113.
[6]Ibid., pp. 130-131.

nations are pledged to regard an armed attack on one member as an attack on all members. NATO represents peace, but it maintains sufficient strength to deter the aggression of communism in the Atlantic Community. President Truman described the treaty well when he stated:

> This treaty is a simple document. The nations which sign it agree to abide by the peaceful principles of the United Nations, to maintain friendly relations and economic cooperation with one another, to consult together whenever the territory or independence of any one of them is threatened, and to come to the aid of any one of them which may be attacked.[7]

The North Atlantic Treaty involved the United States in the affairs of Europe to a degree which would have been unbelievable at the end of World War I. The threat of Communist aggression had supplanted the prejudices of the American people against foreign entanglements with a fear of communism. The sage advice against foreign entanglements given to the nation by its first President had been overtaken by the technology of the era.

KOREA

In August, 1949, the Soviet Union exploded its first atomic bomb some two and one-half years before the United States expected the capability to exist in Russia. This ended the nuclear monopoly of the United States and touched off a nuclear arms race.[8] The nation was face to face with a problem of war which seemed completely

---

[7] US Dept of State, The Signing of the North Atlantic Treaty, p. 33.
[8] Truman, op. cit., p. 306.

insolvable--a race which was likely to lead to the total destruction of the Western civilization without any opportunity for a political solution.

In the early morning hours of 25 June 1950, in Korea, the Communists added the direct approach to their familiar tactics of subversion. The North Korean Army launched an unprovoked attack across the 38th Parallel against the Republic of South Korea. The United States immediately presented the problem to the United Nations with recommendations for Security Council action. The Security Council determined that the action of North Korea constituted a breach of the peace, called for an immediate cessation of hostilities, and recall of the North Korean forces back to the 38th Parallel.[9]

When the Security Council called for the members of the United Nations to provide assistance in repelling the aggressors, the President sent ground forces into action to assist the Korean Army. He further ordered the Seventh Fleet to insure the neutrality of Formosa. Air support for the South Korean Army had been furnished previously by the United States.[10]

The majority of the troops in the United Nations military force were provided by the United States; however, the fact that the force was designated as the United Nations force did much to preserve the influence of the newly formed organization. President Truman's determination to react against the Communist attack in Korea through

---

[9]US Dept of State, Office of Public Affairs, United States Policy in the Korean Crisis, pp. 11-17.
[10]Truman, op. cit., pp. 332-345.

the United Nations strengthened the position of the United States

leadership of the non-Communist nations. His decisions were

politically sound, but the United States found that the initial

military response was inadequate and nearly met with early disaster.

The importance of a capable, diversified military organization

was emphasized again by experience. Reliance upon a super-weapon

as the primary means of deterrence was exposed as dangerous.

SUMMARY

The contents of this chapter have provided a few examples of

the foreign policy of the United States after World War II. The

United States did not hide its head in the sand and ignore the

remainder of the world. A genuine effort was made to assist the

needy nations of all continents in the development of a viable

economy and government. The need for alliances with friendly nations

was recognized, and the position of the armed forces in these

alliances gained in importance as the differences between East and

West became more serious. The smaller developing nations were

constantly in danger of being absorbed by the Communist bloc. This

also held true for established nations which were in the process of

regaining their prewar position in the world society. The President's

action in utilizing the American military to insure the freedom of

South Korea served as a message to the world that the United States

was prepared to defend the freedom of all peoples.

The Korean War presented the American military with its first

experience in limited war. Previously the military had been primarily concerned with the destruction of the enemy; however, this war was different. Political considerations had become the partner of military operations in the limited war situation. The tremendous nuclear power developed by the United States and the Soviet Union curtailed the options of operations on the battlefield, and victory became a combination of political and military success. Military victory alone no longer was sufficient to insure success.

CHAPTER 6

CONCLUSIONS

In 1812 the United States was an emerging, underdeveloped nation in comparison to the great powers of France and Great Britain. Less than one-half of the continental United States had been settled, and the young nation was isolated from the problems and intrigues of the European countries. Today the United States is the richest and most powerful nation in the world.

Changes of great magnitude have taken place in the past one hundred and fifty years, and these changes have influenced the actions of the United States. America is thoroughly entangled in the affairs of the world, and the free nations of the west would be pawns in the hands of the Communists in event the United States reverted to its old policy of isolation. The nation is no longer isolated from Europe or any part of the world. It is a part of a close, responsive world which reverberates instantly when any state, no matter how small, becomes involved in an international disturbance. The safety of the protective Oceans on both the east and west coasts no longer exists. The primary consideration is the security of the United States, and the elimination of the natural obstacle of the oceans transports America into European and Asian affairs with devastating speed.

The compression of time by the modern technology of the era has cast aside the protective shield of Europe from around America, and alliances with European states have increased in importance since the end of World War II. The alliances are important for the security of the western European nations; however, they are also important to the United States to insure satisfactory balancing of power between East and West.

During the first one hundred years of American history, the armed forces exerted little influence on the foreign diplomacy of the United States. Near the end of the nineteenth century Theodore Roosevelt became aware of the importance of a strong navy and the influence such a navy would have upon the rest of the world. Although military power did not directly influence the diplomacy of the United States in its negotiations with Spain prior to the Spanish American War, its presence was felt in the peace negotiations. In this war, as well as in World War I which followed, the armed forces were used as a continuation of diplomacy rather than an integral part of it.

Prior to World War II the United States initiated mobilization of the armed forces, and the US Navy was utilized to escort convoys of transport ships carrying cargo between the United States and Iceland. This act integrated the armed forces into the foreign diplomacy of the United States by clearly demonstrating to the Axis powers that any hostile action against United States shipping in the area described above would result in immediate reaction by the US Navy.

The armed forces have become an integral part of the diplomatic team of the United States since World War II. The reduced size of the world, together with the massive power capabilities of both

52

East and West, make it imperative that close, continuous coordination in foreign affairs matters be maintained between the professional diplomat and the professional military establishments.

There are numerous ways in which the military can assist in carrying out the diplomatic mission of the United States, and the means available are not restricted to military operations in combat. The influence that the United States forces exert on the states of Eastern Europe and the Soviet Union in the implementation of the North Atlantic Treaty has served to deter Communist aggression against the states of Western Europe. The positioning of United States forces in Europe as a part of the NATO military organization has provided tangible evidence that the use of force by the Soviet Union in Western Europe would be costly. Actual employment of military forces in armed combat does not negate diplomatic negotiations; however, once a conflict commences between two states, the number of alternatives available to the negotiators is reduced. As the conflict progresses each nation will attempt to reach agreement at a time when its military forces have the advantage.

The importance of the armed forces in carrying out the foreign policies of the United States has increased continually since the end of World War II. The reasons for this increase in military importance in American diplomacy are based upon the change of United States foreign policy from isolation to collective security. As the United States entered into treaty agreements with states throughout the world, the requirement for economic and military assistance for these states increased, and the need for military advice and support to deter Communist aggression assumed greater importance.

The United States forces are well qualified to provide the military assistance required by the developing states. In providing such assistance, the military forces can effectively influence the state receiving assistance in a manner advantageous to the United States. This does not change the primary role of the military; however, its use has been tempered by the massive nuclear potential in the world. The military is a political instrument which can assist in the attainment of the national objectives of the United States by peaceful means. The peaceful settlement of disputes has become increasingly more important to the United States in recent years. Adequate care must be taken in the settlement of disputes between states to insure that the possibility of a nuclear holocaust is kept to a minimum. To accomplish this, the military must be informed of the diplomatic policies of the United States, and the missions assigned to the military forces must be interpreted in accordance with the known foreign policy.

Peace is evasive. As the time and space factors in the world decrease and the countries of the world move closer together, the military establishment must accept its responsibility for assisting in the conduct of foreign affairs. The armed forces must become familiar with the international relations between the United States and the country in which they are located. A close understanding between the armed forces and the diplomatic establishment will assist

in the continuation of peace and successful diplomatic relations
with the countries of the world.

PAUL N. HORTON
Colonel, Infantry